IMAGES
of America

THE BELL
BOMBER PLANT

The Bell Aircraft plant appears here not long after its completion in 1943. In the distance looking north is Kennesaw Mountain, the scene of a fierce Civil War battle. The tarmac would soon be lined with B-29 Superfortress bombers, and the wooded area at lower right would later give way to the Dobbins Air Reserve Base taxiways and apron. (Bill Kinney.)

ON THE COVER: Pres. Franklin D. Roosevelt described the United States as "the arsenal of democracy," and it was obvious he had scenes like the one on the cover of this book in mind as he uttered those words. By the time this photograph was taken late in World War II inside the Bell Aircraft plant in Marietta, Georgia, the 28,000 people employed there were rolling out two copies per day of the biggest, fastest, and most technologically advanced airplane ever built to that point—the B-29 Superfortress bomber. (Kennesaw State University Archives.)

IMAGES
of America

THE BELL
BOMBER PLANT

Joe Kirby

ARCADIA
PUBLISHING

Published by Arcadia Publishing
Charleston SC, Chicago IL, Portsmouth NH, San Francisco CA

Printed in the United States of America

Library of Congress Catalog Card Number: 2008931751

For all general information contact Arcadia Publishing at:
Telephone 843-853-2070
Fax 843-853-0044
E-mail sales@arcadiapublishing.com
For customer service and orders:
Toll-Free 1-888-313-2665

Visit us on the Internet at www.arcadiapublishing.com

To my father, Joseph F. Kirby, who as a sergeant in the Signal Corps of the U.S. Army Air Forces was positioned with his unit between two airstrips full of B-29 Superfortress bombers on the island of Ie Shima off of Okinawa; To my wife, Fran, and children, Lucy and Miles; to the readers of the Marietta Daily Journal; and to the tens of thousands of men and women who spent World War II building B-29s and flying them.

CONTENTS

ACKNOWLEDGMENTS

This book would not have been possible without the contributions and advice from its two main sources. *Marietta Daily Journal* associate editor Bill Kinney worked at the Bell plant in its publicity department fresh out of high school. Not only did he retain a substantial collection of original photographs of the plant, he was also the recipient of plant manager James V. Carmichael's photograph collection, most of them unpublished until now, which Carmichael bequeathed to Kinney not long before his death. Kinney has been an invaluable source of advice, suggestions, and insights about the plant and the history of that era.

My other major source was Dr. Tom Scott, history professor at Kennesaw State University (KSU) and author of *Cobb County, Georgia, and the Origins of the Suburban South*. Dr. Scott was able some years ago to transfer a substantial number of Bell plant–related items from the Bell headquarters in New York to KSU, where they now reside in the college archives. The assistance provided by KSU archive director Dr. Tamara Livingston and her staff also is deeply appreciated.

Also sharing their photographic archives were chairman (and retired Lockheed president) Bob Ormsby and Lori Cowie of the planned Aviation Museum and Discovery Center in Marietta. Thanks go as well to director Dan Cox of the Marietta Museum of History.

This book also includes a previously unpublished photograph of Gen. Lucius D. Clay, who was instrumental in the development of the plant. It was loaned by his grandson, Chuck Clay of Marietta.

Special thanks must go to *Marietta Daily Journal* chief photographer Thinh D. Nguyen for his technical advice and for laboriously rephotographing the Carmichael Collection, which could not otherwise have been reproduced because of its being in a one-of-a-kind limited-edition leather binding.

A final word of thanks must go to the men and women of the Bell photograph department during the war, who did such a superb job of documenting what happened there.

INTRODUCTION

The story of the Bell Aircraft plant in Marietta, Georgia, better known as "The Bell bomber plant," is a study in transformation. It's the story of how leaders in a backwater town decided to build a commercial airfield to catch the overflow from Eastern Airlines' budding Atlanta operation and how on the eve of the United States' entry into World War II, they leveraged the planned airfield to help snare one of the biggest industrial prizes of the crash rearmament drive mounted by Pres. Franklin D. Roosevelt—a massive aircraft assembly plant, the biggest industrial complex ever built in the South. Tens of thousands of workers, very few of them with manufacturing experience, would go on to build the B-29 Superfortress long-range bomber.

In 1940, the site of the future plant was cotton fields and pines. By 1944, it was the largest factory in the Southeast, providing 28,000 jobs. Those fields that had been plowed by mules and barefoot sharecroppers in 1940 were by 1944 churning out hundreds of copies of the world's most complex plane ever built to that point, one that actually used a crude analog computer to help control its machine-gun turrets.

The B-29 Superfortress provided the Army Air Forces with a weapon that could fly farther, faster, and higher and carry a heavier bomb load than any other plane previously built. It was explicitly designed to traverse the vastness of the Pacific and pummel Japan into submission. The two bombers that dropped the atomic bombs on Japan were not built in Marietta but were identical in almost every way to the 668 planes that were.

Construction of the $73-million plant in Marietta started six months before the Boeing-built prototype of the Superfortress, the XB-29, flew for the first time in September 1942. Three summers later, the skies over Japan were filled with nearly 4,000 B-29s, and the fire they rained on the cities below finally brought to an end the bloodiest war the world had ever known.

Yet the B-29 almost was not built at all. Many officers of all branches of the service in the late 1930s felt strategic bombers were a costly and unproven concept and that defense dollars could be better spent on conventional weapons. It was not until early 1939 in the aftermath of the Munich Conference that FDR and Army Chief of Staff Gen. George Marshall bought into the concept of building large numbers of strategic bombers.

Then, with Hitler rampaging across Europe and Japan threatening war as well, Washington consciously decided to locate its major armaments factories distant from the coasts. Bell Aircraft president Larry Bell of Buffalo, New York, was directed to build in the Atlanta area at a site of his choosing. He picked Marietta because of the lengthy airfield planned there, because the site sat astride the L&N Railroad line, and because it was easily accessible by workers from both Atlanta and Marietta.

The exact dimensions of the plant were kept secret at the time for security reasons, but it was obvious to all that there had never been another building of its size built in the Deep South. The main assembly building, known as B-1 and boasting two parallel final assembly lines each a half-mile long, was a staggering 3.2 million square feet in dimension, and the total size of the entire complex came to 4.2 million square feet.

The B-1 building contained sufficient railroad tracks beneath its roof to have sheltered a dozen passenger trains and was the equivalent of 63 football fields in dimension. As was boasted at the time, it had room for 20 battleships, 69 submarines, and 24 PT boats.

The B-1 building is 2,000 feet long by 1,024 feet wide. Its ceiling is four-and-a-half stories above the floor, and because of the huge wingspan of the B-29s to be assembled within, the interior supports had to be widely spaced. Construction of the plant's steel superstructure began September 1, 1942, and ultimately some 32,000 tons of steel were used.

With the possibility of nighttime air raids on this country a distinct fear, it was designed as a "blackout" facility with no windows so that work could proceed 24 hours a day without having to worry about being spotted from the air.

That "no-window" decision meant an alternative method had to be found to provide ventilation. It was crucial to keep the plant's temperature at a constant level to prevent metal components of the planes from expanding, contracting, and warping. And Georgia's sweltering summers were a consideration as well.

The solution was air-conditioning—a rarity in the South at the time, usually found only in first-run movie theaters. It ultimately moved 4 million cubic feet of air per minute through the plant, while a separate system in the plant's railroad bay swept smoke and dust from the air where supplies were unloaded.

The Bell plant wrenched Marietta and Cobb County from a cotton economy into the forefront of Southern industrialism almost overnight. Marietta in 1940 had been a rearward-looking, rural backwater where the Civil War—especially the nearby Battle of Kennesaw Mountain—and Reconstruction were still vivid memories. Many in Washington wondered whether rural Southerners were capable of building something as technologically complex as a B-29. But not only did Southerners build the planes, they did such a thorough job that not one of the 668 crashed during its test flight.

Construction of the Bell plant turned Marietta into a boomtown. Its population quickly more than doubled. The influx of new residents—and new attitudes—gave Marietta and Cobb a gigantic head start over other metro Atlanta counties in terms of economic development. Within a few years, the county was the beneficiary of divided highways, additional schools, and a large modern hospital, which the community otherwise might have waited decades to enjoy.

The Bell plant played a key role in the metamorphosis of Marietta and Cobb County, but that development was inextricably linked with the development and opening of the airport whose runway it shares—originally known as Rickenbacker Field after World War I fighter ace Eddie Rickenbacker, who as president of Eastern Airlines was instrumental in making it economically feasible to build the airfield. That runway was later shared not only by Bell and its successor as plant operator, Lockheed-Martin, but also by Dobbins Air Reserve Base and the adjoining Naval Air Station Atlanta.

Among those who worked at the Bell plant was Helen Dortch Longstreet—the octogenarian widow of Confederate general James Longstreet. She was but the best known (and likely the oldest) of thousands of women at the plant doing what in quieter times had been considered men's work. And the Bell plant offered the best-paying jobs most of the local black community had ever seen, even though most of them were in menial slots and the company apparently had a quota system.

Among the celebrities who visited Bell during the war were comedian Bob Hope, golfer Bobby Jones, entertainer Al Jolson, and future first lady Mamie Eisenhower.

This is the story of visionary and opportunistic leaders who saw the chance to snare an airfield and then a major industrial plant and grabbed for all they were worth. And it is the story of the thousands of "Rosie the Riveters" and of the semi-literate farmers too old to fight who worked as a team to build the most high-tech plane in Franklin D. Roosevelt's "Arsenal of Democracy."

This is the story of the Bell bomber plant.

One

THE MISSION

As 1940 dawned, World War II was already under way in Europe, and it was almost a foregone conclusion that the United States would eventually be drawn into the war as well. So this country was in the early stages of a crash rearmament program, including the first peacetime draft in the nation's history. That effort not only saw the government-funded construction of 450 airports across the country—ostensibly for civilian use—but also stepped-up design and production of military aircraft for the United States' outmoded air force.

The situation was so dire that the government directed arms manufacturers to work together to speed up the process—even to the extent of sharing secrets and prodding companies that designed weapons to let other companies help build them. Such was the case with the newest bomber on the drawing board, designed by the Boeing Corporation to be bigger and faster and carry a bigger payload over longer distances than even the well-known B-17 Flying Fortress. Boeing's new plane, the B-29 Superfortress, would be built not just by Boeing, but by the Glenn Martin Company and Bell Aircraft.

Bell was a small fish in the world of aviation, having only one small plant in Buffalo, New York, at the time, specializing in single-engine fighters, not four-engine bombers. The fact that it wound up building its bomber plant in then-rural Marietta, Georgia, resulted primarily from the efforts of four men: Mayor Rip Blair, Cobb County commissioner George McMillan, county attorney James V. Carmichael, and then-Major Lucius D. Clay, a Marietta native and son of late U.S. senator Alexander Stephens Clay of Marietta, who, as luck would have it, was stationed at the time in Washington, D.C., as the de facto head of the government's airport construction push under the auspices of the Civil Aeronautics Administration.

Ground-breaking for the Bell Plant took place on March 30, 1942—barely three months after Bell chose the Marietta site. And the plant was completed just 54 weeks after the ground-breaking, despite severe war-related shortages of steel and other materials needed.

The future runway at the Bell plant is dotted with tree stumps in this picture from 1941. County leaders prevailed on Washington in June 1941 to fund construction of a large, paved airfield, one of 450 planned by the War Department on the eve of Pearl Harbor. Plans for the Bell plant did not materialize until after work had started on the runway. (Aviation Museum.)

The plant was built on what until 1942 was a checkerboard of cotton fields and pine groves and home to a community of about two dozen black farming families known as Jonesville. The remains of one such farmstead is in the foreground here in this photograph taken May 1 of that year, as bulldozers in the distance begin work on the runway. (Bill Kinney.)

These four, with future general Lucius Clay of Marietta (not pictured), were primarily responsible for bringing the airport to Cobb. From left to right are World War I fighter ace Eddie Rickenbacker (president of Eastern Airlines), county attorney James V. Carmichael, Mayor Rip Blair, and Cobb commissioner George McMillan. With the country still at peace, Rickenbacker agreed to pay Cobb County $25 each time one of his planes used the airfield. (Bill Kinney.)

Ground-breaking for the plant took place on March 30, 1942—less than four months after Pearl Harbor and barely two months after Bell announced plans to build its massive plant. On hand were Bell officials, local dignitaries, and Army Air Corps officers. Note the photographer at lower right. (Bill Kinney.)

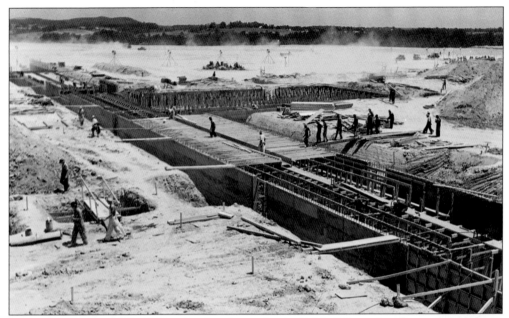

Clouds of dust rise in July 1942 as the foundation for the B-1 building takes shape. Construction proceeded so fast that many concrete walls and support footings were poured before excavation of the plant's basement was complete. The result was that excavation equipment would no longer fit into the areas still to be excavated, which meant that mule-drawn equipment hired from nearby farmers had to be used. (Kennesaw State University Archives.)

In 1940, though just an army major, Marietta native Lucius D. Clay was de facto head of FDR's emergency plan to build 450 airfields—and made sure one was built in his hometown. From left to right in 1943 are Betty Rose Clay, Marjorie Clay, General Clay, and army logistics chief Gen. Brehon Somerville. It was Somerville who conceived and oversaw construction of the Pentagon. (Chuck Clay.)

The first steel column for the soon-to-be massive B-1 building (which would house the main assembly line) is pounded into the ground on September 1, 1942. Some 32,000 tons of steel were used to build the plant, even though it was in extremely short supply because of the war. The plant's final cost was $72 million—coincidentally, the same amount spent to build the Pentagon at the same time. (Bill Kinney.)

Foundation work continues and dust rises in the distance as the runways are graded. The plant was designed by the architectural firm of Robert and Company of Atlanta, which also supervised the construction under the overall auspices of the Army Corps of Engineers. More than 100 contractors and their crews worked 24 hours a day to complete the plant in under a year. (Kennesaw State University Archives.)

The plant's skeleton was beginning to take shape by the time this picture was taken in mid-November 1942. With much of the nation's armaments industry sited along the coasts and vulnerable to air and naval attack, the War Department deliberately chose inland locations for its B-29 plants. Others were built by Boeing in Wichita, Kansas, and Renton, Washington, and by the Glenn Martin Company in Omaha, Nebraska. (Bill Kinney.)

A photograph taken from almost the same location a few months later shows the B-1 building's exterior nearing completion. Close examination of this photograph and others taken during the construction process indicates that a substantial portion of the labor was performed by black workmen, such as these brick masons. (Kennesaw State University Archives.)

This close-up shows a work crew—several of whose members were black—manhandling the scaffolding components up the facade of the 2,000-foot-long, 1,024-foot-wide B-1 main assembly building. That steel-reinforced building, and the other major units of the plant complex, were built as "blackout facilities," meaning they were built without windows so that production could continue 24 hours a day without having to worry about them being visible from the skies by enemy bombers. The lower portion of the four-and-a-half-story building's walls was faced with brick, and the upper portion was covered with corrugated asbestos siding. All of the walls were insulated with two inches of glass wool. The asbestos siding tiles were removed and replaced in the mid-1990s. (Bill Kinney.)

Meanwhile, work was falling behind on the runways. Final approval came from Washington in June 1941 to build a pair of heavy runways—one of 6,000 feet and one of 5,000. Work on them had already started, but as it turned out, they were in the wrong locations, and thus the site had to be regraded from scratch. Nonetheless, construction on the two runways was complete just six months after this picture of the muddy site was snapped. (Bill Kinney.)

Acres of fresh concrete have now replaced the muddy fields shown above. This view was taken from the roof of the B-1 building looking southeast toward the runway visible just beyond the trees. Low on the horizon is Mount Wilkinson in the Vinings area. (Kennesaw State University Archives.)

16

Finished at last in the spring of 1943, the B-1 building gleams in the Georgia sun almost as if it had been polished. In an ultimate tribute to the men who designed and built it, it is still in use six decades later by Lockheed Martin as one of the world's foremost aerospace assembly plants. (Kennesaw State University Archives.)

The B-2, or administration building, was the nerve center of the Bell complex and is seen here nearing completion. Note the enclosed walkways leading to the B-1 building, just visible at left. Not as substantial as the rest of the plant, B-2 outlived its usefulness despite several renovations and was eventually demolished in 2007. (Kennesaw State University Archives.)

At right is the paint shop, into which newly assembled Superfortress bombers would be towed and then painted. But due to the delays in the program and a desire to lighten the aircraft, Washington ultimately decreed the B-29s would do without the camouflage paint, saving several thousand pounds. In the distance is Blackjack Mountain, and barely visible in the distance is Sweat Mountain at the Cobb-Fulton County line. (Bill Kinney.)

The B-4 building, at which final assembly and cleanup of the bombers would take place, is nearly complete in this April 1943 photograph. Bell was in such a hurry to get the plant up and running that initial assembly on the first bomber began even before the buildings were complete. Night shift workers later recalled being able to look up and see the stars and recalled getting wet when it rained because the roof wasn't finished. (Bill Kinney.)

Another shot of the B-4 building was taken a month or so later. At left, sporting a brick facade, are the flight control building and tower. Note the worker on the ladder high up on the far left of the building near the roof, apparently working on the building's siding. (Bill Kinney.)

It was vital that the plant's temperature be kept stable to prevent metal plane components from expanding, contracting, and warping. So in an era when air-conditioning was a rarity, the plant was air-conditioned. These are some of the 99 ventilators on the roof of the B-1 building that helped move 4 million cubic feet of air per minute through the plant. (Bill Kinney.)

Seen above are the front of the B-3 Paint Shop Building and the rear of the B-4 Final Assembly Building as construction nears completion. The Bell bomber complex was so big that a steam plant was constructed just to serve it. Comprising more than 4 million square feet, the factory was the biggest industrial facility south of the Mason-Dixon Line and was double the size of the Bell plant in Niagara, New York. The Bell power plant is seen below. More than six decades later it is still in use, helping power Lockheed Martin's assembly of F-22 Raptor fighters, C-130J Hercules cargo planes, and other aircraft. (Both Bill Kinney.)

A cadre of Bell executives and others moved to Marietta from Niagara, but most of its workforce was recruited locally. Bell initially opened an employment office in the Rhodes-Haverty Building in downtown Atlanta while the plant was under construction before opening this employment office on-site in the fall of 1943. The building also served as the plant's infirmary. (Bill Kinney.)

One of the reasons Bell chose Marietta for the plant was the fact that the L&N Railroad (today the CSX) ran right through town, providing an easy way to ship materials to the plant in the pre-interstate era. This photograph was taken looking south from the plant toward Fair Oaks. (Bill Kinney.)

An additional 8 miles worth of spur lines were laid from the main line into the new Bell plant, including the rails being put down by the crew in this picture. In the background are the as-yet-unopened employment office at left, the power plant at center, and the B-1 building at right. (Bill Kinney.)

Two of the plant's diesel locomotives are shown here. The smaller engine at right was a product of the Plymouth Locomotive Works in Plymouth, Ohio, which built more than 7,500 smaller-scale locomotives between 1910 and the 1990s. Incidentally, the Bell plant was directly across South Cobb Drive from the Glover Machine Works factory, which manufactured more than 200 small-scale steam locomotives between 1902 and 1930. (Kennesaw State University Archives.)

Col. Charles W. O'Connor, left, hands the symbolic key to the plant to Capt. Harry Collins, the plant's first general manager, on April 15, 1943, signifying the plant's completion. The ground-breaking for the South's largest manufacturing plant had taken place 54 weeks earlier. (Kennesaw State University Archives.)

Though the exterior of B-1 was complete when this picture was taken, much work remained on the inside before aircraft assembly could take place. The plant's emptiness emphasizes just how vast its interior space is—both then and now, the biggest aircraft assembly building in the world under one roof. (Kennesaw State University Archives.)

This is the calm before the storm. The future flight-line assembly area of the B-1 building is almost empty of people and devoid of aircraft components. Within months, it will be filled with bombers in the process of assembly. (Kennesaw State University Archives.)

A group of Bell officials, including one and possibly two women, walks toward what soon will be the final assembly area for the B-29 in May 1943. The huge plant dwarfs the few people in view—and soon will dwarf the airplanes built there as well. (Bill Kinney.)

Cafeterias for the Bell workers were scattered throughout the plant, but there were a pair of special dining areas in the B-2 administration building for the company brass. Seen above is a section of the executive dining room, boasting white tablecloths and floral arrangements on the tables; and in the other picture, the guest dining room at which company officials entertained visiting brass from Washington, visiting stars from Hollywood, and Bell brass from the headquarters in Buffalo. The food service department at Bell was headed by Lorena Pruitt, who a year following the war's conclusion became the first woman ever elected to political office in Cobb when she successfully ran for mayor of Smyrna in 1946. (Both Bill Kinney.)

Important visitors to the Bell plant entered via this lobby in the B-2 administration building. The plaque on the wall reads: "Bell Bomber Plant, Marietta, Ga.; Major W. A. Feret, Area Engineer, Corps of Engineers; Designed and Constructed by Robert and Company Associates; Architects, Engineers, Managers; Atlanta, Georgia; 1943." The company was still one of the Atlanta area's premiere design firms as this book was being written more than 65 years later. The building included swank offices for company president Larry Bell, Marietta mayor Rip Blair, and county attorney James V. Carmichael, who later was hired as the plant's manager. Carmichael is seen below at his desk with Army Air Forces Col. Charles W. O'Connor (left). Company president Bell split his time between Buffalo and Marietta during the war. (Both Bill Kinney.)

Night falls on Marietta's economic past in this photograph, as a new era of unimaginable prosperity is signified by the plant on the hill. The plowed field in the foreground—like most of its counterparts around Cobb County—will soon give way to houses, apartments, fast-food restaurants, and asphalt, all fueled by the arrival of the Bell plant. (Bill Kinney.)

The Rickenbacker Training School was set up by a New Deal agency, the National Youth Administration, and later taken over by Cobb County. And Bell set up a training office in downtown Atlanta while construction of the plant was under way. Here an aspiring "Rosie the Riveter" practices as her instructor looks on. Riveting was a two-person job: note the pair of legs facing "Rosie." (Bill Kinney.)

Two

REVVING UP

One of the reasons the Atlanta area was chosen for the Bell plant was the low cost of land. Another was the sizeable reservoir of unemployed and underemployed people there. Yet by the time the plant was nearing completion, many of them had found other work or been drafted. In addition, many were reluctant to work for Bell due to the assumption that it would close when the war ended (not a misplaced fear, as it turned out).

Bell's answer was to hire women. The ranks of Rosie the Riveters at the plant topped out at 37 percent in early 1945. Women filled an array of jobs at the plant, from security guard to crane operator.

The opportunities for African American workers were more limited. Though Bell had just over 2,000 blacks on its payroll in January 1945, it apparently had a quota system, as no more than 800 were ever in skilled-labor positions. And even those fortunate enough to obtain the higher-paying skilled-labor work found themselves shunted into segregated working areas and assembly lines. Though Bell was Northern-owned, the plant maintained separate restrooms and water fountains for blacks and whites, as was common all over the South in that era.

Yet the bomber plant represented a step toward better employment opportunities for blacks. Some were hired for skilled-labor positions, and even menial workers had the opportunity to earn more than ever before.

Bell also employed a number of midgets and/or dwarves, chosen because they could squeeze into spaces where a full-sized adult could not. And the plant employed 1,750 disabled workers, according to plant manager Jimmie Carmichael, who himself was severely disabled as a result of an auto accident as a teen. Carmichael relied on canes, a wheelchair, and motorized carts to get around the plant.

Among the disabled working at the bomber plant were blind workers whose job it was to sort by hand the stray rivets that were swept up from the plant floor. And as predicted, many Bell hires did come from farming backgrounds. But most farmers had experience working on farm machines—and they were no strangers to hard work.

With gasoline and tires subject to wartime rationing, many Bell employees walked to work. Those who lived further away shared rides. Thousands of others commuted via the old interurban trolley line that ran from Atlanta to Marietta Square and stopped at the plant. And the government built Cobb County's first four-lane divided highway from Atlanta to the plant to make it more accessible. That road—U.S. 41, today's Cobb Parkway—is still referred to as "The Four Lane" by older Mariettans. Once at work, it was impractical to leave to run errands because of security and transportation restrictions, so the plant featured numerous cafeterias and stores for employees. A sale seems to have been under way at the store seen below, with one of the featured items a pith helmet of the type worn by some of the plant's security guards. (Both Bill Kinney.)

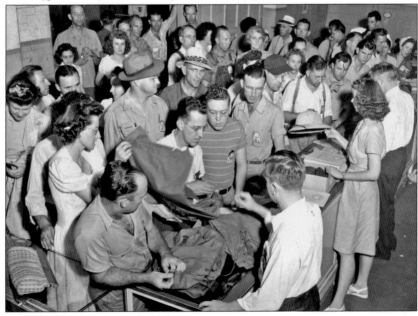

Wartime rationing meant the military got first call on everything. Residents would pick up their ration books from government offices in downtown Marietta and Atlanta. The Bell plant drew workers from as far as Murphy, North Carolina, and they were entitled to supplemental ration coupons for gas and tires because they were doing vital wartime work. Housing was in short supply as well. Thousands of Bell workers moved into the Marietta Place public housing project on Fairground Street and into small houses and duplexes that sprung up within walking distance of the plant. (Both Bill Kinney.)

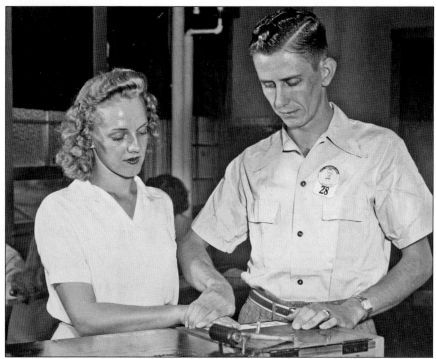

Prospective hires at the Bell Aircraft plant underwent fingerprinting, and higher-ranking employees were subject to background checks, all part of the wartime effort to safeguard security at crucial defense plants. Such efforts ultimately proved both successful and unnecessary, as there were no known efforts by employees at Bell to sabotage production or steal secrets. Bell employees who faced work-related or personal problems were encouraged to meet with one of the plant's personnel counselors, one of whom, Mildred Allen, is seen below. This shot probably dates from the spring of 1944 or 1945 judging by the vase of fresh jonquils on Allen's desk. (Both Bill Kinney.)

As with many industrial plants of Bell's size, there was substantial medical infrastructure in place. This pair of 1942-model Buick Flexible Ambulances stood ready to roll at a moment's notice in case of accident on the runway or in the plant. Note the sirens on their roofs. (The "Flexible" part of the ambulance's name stemmed from the fact that the vehicles could double as hearses.) The plant also featured a dispensary in the same building as the Employment Office, at which employees could see a doctor, get shots, get an X-ray, or have their teeth checked, as seen below. (Both Bill Kinney.)

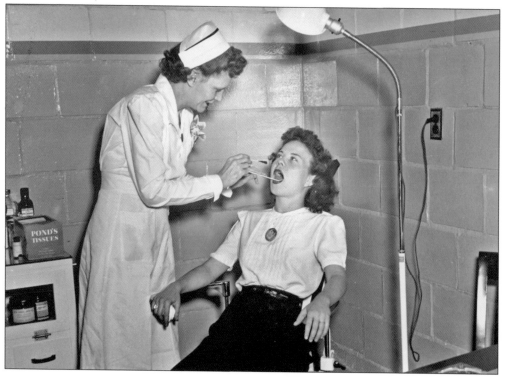

Bell hired hundreds of men and women to work as security guards for the sprawling plant and runway, which encompassed hundreds of acres. Some 132 of those guards are seen in the picture below. Close examination shows that many of them were overweight and/or overage—but such was to be expected when most young men were in the service. The scarcity of able-bodied men no doubt was a reason why the plant also hired females to work as guards. A half dozen of them are in the picture below, but they are all but invisible, as they were lined at the rear of the formation. Nonetheless, at least one of the plant's female guards—the one depicted above on the plant's firing range with her male colleagues—was allowed to carry a firearm in the course of her duties. (Both Bill Kinney.)

Most of those hired by Bell had never worked in an industrial setting, and most had never used a time clock. Yet they flocked to Marietta from around the state, lured by the prospect of earning 60¢ an hour. Many came from farming backgrounds, and a fairly substantial part of the workforce was illiterate, which meant they signed their timecards and endorsed their paychecks with a mark rather than their name. Above is an office full of Bell's timekeepers, who sat day after day poring over the company's timecards. Below is one of the men who ran the company's automated check-writing machine. At the plant's peak employment during the war, the payroll topped $1 million per week—an enormous boost for the Marietta and Atlanta economies that just a couple years before had still been in the throes of the Great Depression. (Both Bill Kinney.)

During the year the plant was under construction, Bell trained the workers it was hiring. Some were sent to the company plant at its headquarters in Buffalo, New York, while special schools were set up in downtown Atlanta and Marietta for others. It is unclear where this photograph of supervisory trainees was snapped. The writing on the blackboard reads, "Local elastic failures," and includes a pair of complex formulas. (Bill Kinney.)

E-mail and text messaging devices were the kinds of gizmos that could only be found in Dick Tracy cartoons in the 1940s, so the plant relied heavily on the telephone. The Bell plant's initial order from Bell Telephone for the plant was for 900 phones—a number that only increased through the years. Switchboard operators like these helped place 35,000 calls a day at the plant. (Bill Kinney.)

It was the job of these women to keep Bell's office supplies in stock—everything from such mundane items as paper and pens to specialized tools like slide rules and graph paper. It was the Rosie the Riveters who got the glory, but plenty of other women spent the war doing tedious, thankless jobs like this. (Bill Kinney.)

In the days before modern copy machines, the only way to mass-produce for wide consumption certain large-scale documents like this blueprint was to photograph them, then make copies of the print. This blueprint reads, in part, "Details of Typical Prefabricated Panels for Shops," as in the different preassembly areas of the plant. (Bill Kinney.)

Morale posters were considered indispensable to maintaining the spirits of those in the front lines and those on the home front—so vital that the Bell plant maintained its own in-house unit to produce them. Among those on view here is one that exhorts, "59 Bombers Lost! They Need B-29 Bombers Now!" and another that states, "Congratulations to All Bell Employees: Let's Stay On Schedule in '44." (Bill Kinney.)

The Bell factory had an in-house publicity department, seen here, that churned out news releases and a plant newspaper, the *Bell Aircraft News*. Its youngest member, seen here second from left in the front office, was Bill Kinney, 17, who went on to a notable seven-decade career covering Marietta for the *Marietta Daily Journal* and was still working full-time there as this book was written. His photograph collection is the foundation for this book. At far right is reporter Jim Little, spouse of star *Atlanta Journal-Constitution* reporter and columnist Celestine Sibley. (Bill Kinney.)

These are the men (Don Kaufman is at right) who took most of the photographs that grace the pages of this book. They are posed here with their Speed Graphic cameras on the runway apron outside the B-1 building in front of a prewar Ford Woody station wagon that was specially modified for them. (Bill Kinney.)

Bell's photographers did their own darkroom work and printed their own pictures on-site. Their work adorned many of the office walls in the plant, including the print room in their photo lab. On the table in the background are copies of *Life* magazine and other photographic magazines. A larger print of the photograph sits on the table at lower left. For a better view of that image, see page 48. (Bill Kinney.)

The main building at the Bell plant was a half-mile long and a quarter-mile wide, so scores of scooters like those seen here were employed by Bell's Transportation Department to whisk managers, engineers, visiting dignitaries, and others around the plant. More than 600 conveyances of various kinds were in use at the plant, including hundreds of bicycles—or should be stated, "tricycles"—like those seen below, used by company couriers for interplant mail. A courier could easily pedal 50 miles a day through the plant and its office corridors without ever venturing beyond its walls. Bikes like those below are still in use at the plant. (Both Bill Kinney.)

The main building at the plant was nearly a mile from the runway, and the administration building was even farther—a long walk in the Georgia sun. So Bell set up a shuttle service to ferry pilots, company brass, visiting celebrities, and War Department officials back and forth. The drivers seen here helped rack up nearly 1 million miles worth of trips between 1943 and 1945. (Bill Kinney.)

Typing with carbon paper was the standard way of duplicating letters and similar documents in the 1940s and for years to come; but when large numbers of copies were needed, secretaries turned to the "ditto" machine, which could churn out hundreds of copies. From left to right are Lynne Lambert, Eva McRae, Mildred Watson, and Beth Willis. (Kennesaw State University Archives.)

Many workers gathered on their lunch break to sing religious hymns on the broad staircases leading down to the transportation tunnels that run the length of the plant. It was a time when sheet-music arrangements of hit songs sold in the millions, and Americans routinely gathered around the family piano to sing for entertainment. It was a more religious era, and nearly every Bell employee had loved ones and friends in uniform overseas. Seen here are paperback hymnals that have been passed out, although the words no doubt were familiar to many of those singing. And it's not hard to imagine that the man leading this informal chorus had a second job on Sundays as a preacher or choir director. (Bill Kinney.)

The courtyard between the B-1 (assembly) and B-2 (administration) buildings was turned into a recreation area during lunch breaks on nice days. Seen here are a pair of volleyball games in progress, while off to the sides, various pairs of ball glove–wearing workers—including female ones—toss softballs. (Bill Kinney.)

Shift changes would find 10,000 or so workers headed into the plant while a nearly equal number headed home, such as those pictured here. Workers entered and departed the plant through what were known as "headhouses," where guards checked their identities for espionage and theft. (Kennesaw State University Archives.)

Bell bomber sponsored teams in after-hours baseball and softball leagues playing against other businesses and industries from around the state. Seen here are the Bell Bomberettes, the women's basketball team, which came close to winning the state championship. The men's softball team captured the state crown in 1945. (Bill Kinney.)

Chicago White Sox shortstop and future Hall of Famer Luke Appling (left) spent 1944–1945 in the army playing and helping manage the team fielded by Lawson General Hospital, an army rehabilitation facility in Chamblee. He is seen here before the Lawson-Bell game with (continuing from left to right) minor leaguer Bobby Dews, Johnny Hill, former Philadelphia Phillies outfielder LeGrant Scott, and Pittsburgh Pirates pitcher Pep Rambert. (Bill Kinney.)

Each Superfortress bomber featured four massive engines like this one, a supercharged 18-cylinder Curtiss-Wright R-3350. The engines were manufactured by Pratt and Whitney and shipped by railcar to Marietta and the other three plants around the country where the B-29s were being assembled (Wichita, Kansas, and Renton, Washington, by Boeing, and Omaha, Nebraska, by Martin). Such massive engines were needed to power the long-range bomber across thousands of miles of open ocean, each way, to hit the Japanese mainland. Each engine was capable of 2,200 horsepower at takeoff and 2,300 horsepower at 25,000 feet. All that muscle gave the Superfortress a speed of 350 miles per hour at 40,000 feet. Unfortunately, the early B-29 engines had a tendency to overheat and catch fire because the cowlings that surrounded them were too small and allowed in insufficient air to keep them cool. (Bill Kinney.)

Three

TAKING SHAPE

The Bell plant was notable for a couple of reasons already discussed—its mammoth size and the speed with which it was constructed and put into operation. But it made history in an even more significant way by being one of the first to use an assembly-line approach to building airplanes. Until the B-29 came along, most aircraft were assembled by hand. But because of wartime urgency, and because the War Department envisioned building 700 of the bombers by January 1945, it was decided to build them on an assembly line. Unlike cars, it is impractical to build planes on a conveyer belt. Instead, the parts and components of the B-29 were crafted one item at a time in shops around the edges of the plant, then were transported by pushcart or overhead crane a stop at a time toward the center of the building, where there were a pair of side-by-side final assembly lines stretching the half-mile length of the building. The plant rang with the cacophony of giant steel presses slamming down on aluminum sheets, the screams of drilling machines and metal-cutting saws, and the simultaneous hammering of thousands of compressed-air rivet guns.

Many of those rivet guns were in the hands of Rosie the Riveter and her sisters, but contrary to popular myth, men made up the majority of the workforce.

The Bell plant was slow getting up to speed because of shortages of materials, tools, and labor, and production was hampered as well by thousands of design changes from Boeing's engineers in California, the designers of the plane. The first 14 planes to leave the plant wound up being built mostly by hand. But the first Superfortress finally rolled out of the plant in November 1943—a scant year-and-a-half after ground-breaking for the plant. Another 667 were soon to follow.

One of Bell's diesel engines exits the plant heading toward the junction with the L&N Railroad line, which ran along the western edge of the Bell complex. The proximity of the railroad was a major factor in Bell's selection of the site on which to build the plant. Most of what went into a B-29 arrived via train. (Bill Kinney.)

Railroad tracks ran the length of the mammoth B-1 building. That portion of the plant had a ventilation system separate from the rest of the building, in order that the smoke and dust from the trains could be vented out. Surplus parts for the Superfortress were shipped by rail across the country to the other three plants in which the airplane was being assembled. (Bill Kinney.)

The low-roofed machine shop sat beneath the second-floor mezzanine of the B-1 building. Here men and women labored around the clock to craft small metal parts for the Superfortress. In the distance to the right can be seen the broad expanse of the main assembly area of the plant. (Bill Kinney.)

Another view of the machine maintenance shop is pictured. Washington had feared Southerners would lack the education and the industrial background to master aircraft assembly. But as it turned out, most farmers had plenty of experience working with tools and repairing small machines, and those skills carried over to their work in the plant. (Bill Kinney.)

Although President Roosevelt had been pressured by black leaders into issuing an executive order barring discrimination at defense plants, it had no enforcement powers and only a limited effect. Most jobs available to blacks at the Bell plant were menial, such as those seen here, collecting scrap metal from the plant's floor. (Kennesaw State University Archives.)

Nearly every photograph in this book was taken by Bell photographers, including this staged one that was unfortunately typical of the era. The Bell plant featured segregated cafeterias, bathrooms, and drinking fountains, as was common practice in the South at the time. Yet even those doing menial labor at Bell earned more than they ever had before. (Bill Kinney.)

Though most of the 2,000 or so blacks at Bell worked as laborers, up to 800 were hired for skilled labor positions—although apparently never more than that. These women are dipping various metal components for the B-29 in chemicals as part of the cadmium-plating process. It was a substantial step above menial work but not pleasant—as the looks on the faces of these workers plainly show. (Bill Kinney.)

About 8 percent of Bell's workforce was black in a county where they made up 16 percent of the population. And in most cases, blacks and whites worked in segregated assembly lines—but not all. Pictured here is an intermingled crew attending to a 2,500-ton hydraulic press, which towers over them all. (Bill Kinney.)

A B-29 bomber was equipped with numerous pieces of electronic gear—radios, radar, intercoms, microphones, and headphones—each piece of which had to be tested and checked out before it was installed. Pictured is part of that inspection process under way. Most of the components that went into the plane, including those seen here, were built elsewhere and then shipped to Marietta to be part of the assembly process. The Superfortress was the most technically advanced airplane ever built to that point, and the equipment it carried was equally complex. Its crew was scattered throughout the plane, from nose to tail, which made it vital to have a working intercom for communication. (Bill Kinney.)

Bell's well-equipped on-site chemistry lab took the guesswork out of materials analysis for the Superfortress. A sizeable percentage of the engineers hired by Bell for its lab, and to work in its engineering department, were recent graduates of the nearby Georgia Institute of Technology in Atlanta. (Bill Kinney.)

Chemical materials weren't the only things tested at Bell. This lab featured a pressure chamber in which test-crewmen were subjected to the stratospheric temperatures and pressure conditions they could expect while flying the B-29 at heights of up to 33,000 feet. Note the fleece-lined leather pressure suit and boots in which this test subject is clad. (Bill Kinney.)

The first B-29 built at the plant was assembled almost entirely by hand, as Washington was pressing Bell hard to get production under way. This photograph shows a skeleton crew in the early stages of the process. Note what appears to be a large wooden template on the workbench in the foreground and the emptiness of the plant in the distance. (Bill Kinney.)

Workers in the metal fabrication department share a laugh. The B-29 was designed by Boeing, which shipped its patterns and blueprints to Bell. Then workers like these would use that information to craft the metal components of the plane one by one. The outer edges of the plant floor were lined with workshops like this one. (Kennesaw State University Archives.)

Each B-29 contained 7,000 feet—nearly a mile and a half—of electrical wiring. The wires were unspooled into an extremely intricate web of harnesses stretching through the plane, many of them comprised of 100 to 200 sets of wires each. And each wire was stamped with an ID number so they could be installed in the right places as they were threaded throughout the plane. The work was both demanding and tedious. Yet it turned out to be another case in which the women assembling the electrical harnesses did excellent work, even though few of them had technological or mechanical backgrounds. Many women's hands are both small and dexterous, two qualities advantageous for the work. In the picture above, women are preparing the wires on a workbench. The process continues in the picture below. (Both Bill Kinney.)

Alina Hobbs may have been an engineer but more likely was a draftswoman, making copies of plans. Plant engineers stayed busy reengineering the plane in response to thousands of change orders from Boeing and Washington. Then multitudinous copies of the updated plans had to be dispersed throughout the plant. Note here as well the photo ID on Hobbs's lapel. All Bell workers wore such IDs. (Kennesaw State University Archives.)

These three women worked as metal fabricators and seemed happy to see the photographer come along. Although women workers were numerous at the plant, they never comprised a majority of the workforce, despite the fact that the rapidly expanding armed services had most of the country's young men in uniform. The plant's percentage of women workers topped out at 37 percent in early 1945. (Kennesaw State University Archives.)

Bell worker Mary Withrow operates a spot-welding machine. Many Bell workers had young children, and the Bell plant did not offer on-site day care. Yet the federal government subsidized a large, 24-hour childcare center at the 500-unit Marietta Place apartments just down the hill from the plant. The center was managed by the Marietta school system. (Kennesaw State University Archives.)

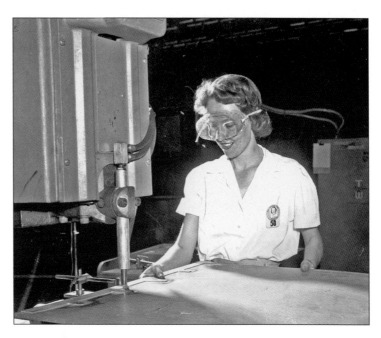

The newly hired Bell workers in this photograph taken in July 1944 were in an orientation class taught by MaNita Dunwody. They are holding booklets titled, "You're A War Worker Now!" On the wall are posters exhorting them to buy war bonds, one of them blaring the message, "Your Vacation Ticket to Victory!" Note the unfinished drywall behind them. (Kennesaw State University Archives.)

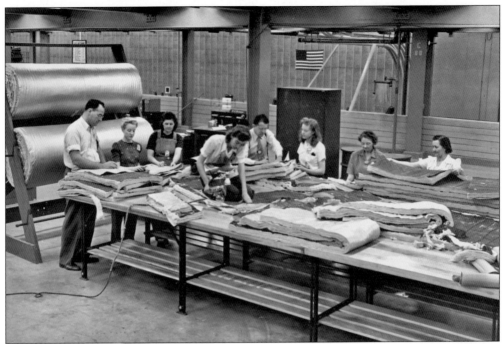

The B-29 was "pressurized," meaning the engine's intake of air would be heated and compressed and the interior of the craft would be sealed from the subzero stratospheric temperatures outside. That meant crews would not need to wear heavy clothing but meant the plane would have to be insulated. Pictured here is a crew cutting strips of insulation that will later be fitted inside the fuselage. (Bill Kinney.)

The Superfortresses were too big to be shipped by rail to their ultimate destination. So they flew, but not until after a test flight over Marietta. And in an ultimate testament to the ability of Bell's workers in Marietta, not one of the 668 planes built there crashed. Here a parachute is being packed in preparation for a test flight. The signs read, "Keep Off Parachute Packing Table." (Bill Kinney.)

The Bell plant had its own foundry. Pictured is a zinc-based alloy (also including aluminum, magnesium, and copper) called Kirksite being poured around plastic patterns. The process allowed for the rapid casting of new parts necessitated by the flood of change orders as the plane was engineered and built. (Bill Kinney.)

This young lady's job was to operate a compressor that would "blow up"—i.e. form—the Plexiglas astrodomes (sometimes referred to at the time as "asterdomes") on the side and top of the B-29's fuselage. The domes gave the plane's machine-gun operators a view of potential attackers—and targets. (Bill Kinney.)

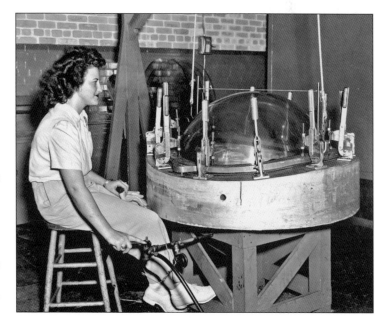

Bell workers produced thousands of astrodomes like those being inspected here. Each was checked for clarity and for strength. Clarity was vital so the gunners would have a clear view of the sky. And ensuring the plastic Plexiglas was sufficiently strong was crucial as well, because flight tests elsewhere had shown that the plane's gunners were at risk of being blown out of the pressurized airplane to their deaths if the astrodome, or "blister," was to come off or be ruptured by gunfire. The flight tests also had shown that the B-29's windows tended to frost over at the stratospheric altitudes at which it was to operate. That meant Boeing engineers had to develop a new kind of glass, as well as design an improved defrost system for installation. (Bill Kinney.)

Finishing touches are put onto eight Curtiss-Wright R-3350 engines. Unfortunately, early models of the engine were prone to overheating and caused fires so intense the wing would burn through in seconds. The 18-cylinder engine also was used to power the Douglas A-1 Skyraider fighter, Douglas DC-7 passenger plane, the Fairchild C-119 Flying Boxcar transport plane, the Lockheed Constellation passenger plane, and the Lockheed P-2 Neptune antisubmarine patrol plane. (Bill Kinney.)

The engines were housed in these units, known as nacelles, which were installed on the B-29's wings. This photograph also offers a good view of the plant's floor, which was composed not of concrete, but of wooden blocks. The blocks were chosen because they made for a softer surface on which to stand during long shifts and because they were easy to remove in order to install hoses and lines as needed. (Bill Kinney.)

Rather than build the plane on a conveyer belt, its components were constructed separately and later assembled by steps. In the foreground above are fuselage sections in a vertical position, while in the background are fuselages further in the construction process that have been lain on their sides. The picture below shows a cutaway view of a fuselage and is a notable reminder of the way the civilian population was mobilized for the war effort, including septuagenarian Berry Hicks at front. An even older worker at the plant was Helen Dortch Longstreet, the octogenarian widow of Confederate general James Longstreet. Helen Longstreet worked as a riveter, and her efforts at the plant were profiled in *Life* magazine during the war. (Both Bill Kinney.)

This is how a fuselage like those on the opposite page looked while under construction before being turned to a horizontal position. Two "Rosies" are applying a pair of the thousands of rivets that will be employed by the time the section is complete. The fuselage was 9 feet, 6 inches wide at its maximum width, and most of it (approximately 40 percent) was devoted to carrying bombs. When complete, it also contained the upper rear turret; the left- and right-hand gunners' sights (or "blisters"); seats for all three gunners; oxygen panels for all three gunners, plus portable oxygen bottles and an auxiliary crew oxygen equipment panel; a computer voltage regulator; an emergency cabin pressure relief valve; crew berths (fixed cots) for napping on long flights; and a toilet. (Bill Kinney.)

A team of riveters is seen on a pressure bulkhead nearing completion that eventually will form one end of a pressurized compartment in the fuselage. Everyone knows about Rosie the Riveter, but most don't realize that riveters worked in teams, just as it is seen here. The woman on the near side of the bulkhead is the riveter, while the woman on the other side was known as the "bucker." The riveter would place a rivet through the predrilled holes in the sheets of metal and then hold an air gun against the rivet's head. The bucker, meanwhile, would push a steel bar up against the end of the rivet on the other side and would hold the bar there until the force of the air gun caused the rivet's head to mushroom into a weld-like binding. It is likely that the man riveting in the picture has an unseen partner acting as bucker on the other side of the bulkhead. Each B-29 contained more than 1 million rivets. (Bill Kinney.)

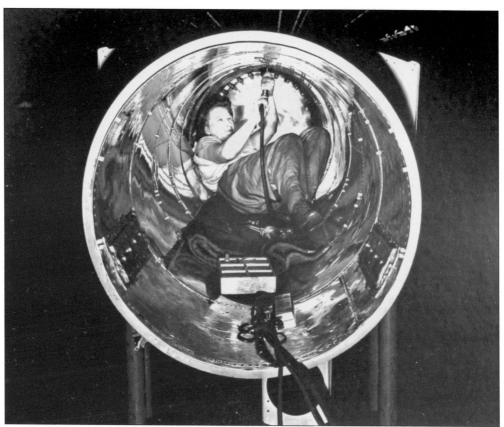

The bomb bay area of the fuselage was not pressurized. So a narrow tunnel—28 inches in diameter and 35 feet long—allowed crewmen to crawl from the nose to the tail without leaving the pressurized area. This woman is riveting the inside of such a tunnel—a task that must have been absolutely deafening. And she doesn't appear to be wearing any sort of ear protection. (Bill Kinney.)

Not only were women prized for certain jobs at Bell for their smaller hands and fingers, but they typically could more easily fit into confined areas than a man could—areas like this one, in which a worker is lacing up braces on one of the fuel cells. Not surprisingly for a plane capable of flying thousands of miles without stopping, the B-29 had a net fuel capacity of 9,501 gallons. (Bill Kinney.)

Riveting proceeds here on wings for the B-29. At this point in the assembly process, the wings were standing vertically (as were the fuselage sections). And that necessitated a two-level approach to the riveting. A close look reveals a row of riveters on the lower level with their backs to the camera. (Bill Kinney.)

Pictured is a wing in the process of being moved by crane to the final assembly point in the wing line. Next will come the attachment of the motors and the nacelles (or motor housings). The B-29's wingspan was gargantuan—some 141 feet, 2.75 inches, with a total area of 1,736 square feet. (Bill Kinney.)

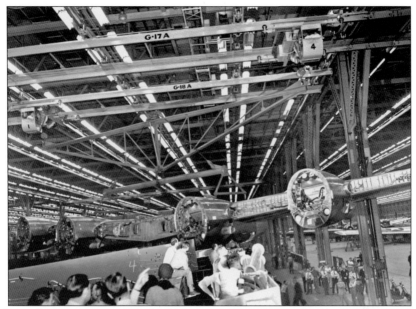

The ceiling of the main assembly building at Bell was latticed with girders that supported numerous cranes, each of which was capable of lifting 10 tons. Yet once the engine nacelles were attached to the wings, the wings weighed 16 tons. The successful solution—as proposed by a Bell employee—was an ingenuous two-crane setup like that seen above being used to move one of the wings. Look closely at the ceiling to see the two crane drivers. At left is Number 1 and at right is Number 4. The picture below is a close-up—a bird's-eye view, one might say—of a crane operator in action. Many of the crane jockeys at Bell were women, who proved quite adept at the work. (Both Bill Kinney.)

The engines have been attached to the nacelles and the nacelles to the wings, and the wings have been attached to the fuselage. And now the propellers are affixed to the motors. Early versions of the B-29 used a three-bladed propeller, but when the plane went into full production, the decision was made to use a more powerful four-bladed model. The propellers were manufactured by the Hamilton Standard Propeller division of United Aircraft Corporation at its plant and were enormous—sporting a diameter of 16 feet, 7 inches. At their lowest point, they were about 2 feet off the ground. And all told, the distance from the ground to the top of a propeller blade on a B-29 was roughly 20 feet, or twice the height of a basketball goal. (Bill Kinney.)

Parts for the nose cone were fabricated in the Bell plant, just as they were for the center wing assembly and tail-gunner's section. This picture shows a number of B-29 nose cabins in various stages of production, from the nearly complete versions at left to the still-skeletal versions at right. And in the rear on the plant floor can be seen the frameworks for several more. (Bill Kinney.)

Cars can be built on conveyer belts, but not giant airplanes like the Superfortress. Instead, the B-29's components were built in various shops around the sides of the plant, then wheeled on pushcarts or, in the case of the main wing spars like the one dangling in this picture over a row of fuselage compartments, lugged by crane to the final assembly area. (Kennesaw State University Archives.)

The process of building a B-29 was incredibly loud. The sounds of thousands of compressed-air guns hammering rivets mixed with the thunder of giant presses slamming on aluminum and the metal-on-metal screech from dozens of drilling machines and cutting machines created a cacophony of noise. Few, if any, Bell workers wore ear protection. This riveter and bucker working inside a wing communicated by intercom. (Bill Kinney.)

The B-29's tail, wing sections, and engines were manufactured elsewhere then shipped to Marietta. Here the finishing touches are being put on a tail section, which towers high above the plant's floor. Although the plane's main landing gear was under the nose and big wings, the Superfortress also sported a small wheel on the tail for use in case the nose became too elevated during takeoff. (Bill Kinney.)

This tail section is just starting down the half-mile-long final assembly line. The goal is the tiny patch of white just to right of the top of the fin—the exit door. Just ahead are three tail wings with the dorsal (upright) fin yet to be attached. Still to be added to the tail in the foreground are the tail-gunner's compartment and the rudder. (Bill Kinney.)

This Superfortress is about ready to hit the runway. All four of its engines and nacelles are attached and three of its four propellers. In front on the floor are four other motors, all on wheeled platforms, being worked on. Chances are they were headed toward the next Superfortress in line, which can be seen just behind the one in front and which lacks both nacelles and engines. Note what might be disc-shaped nose sections or perhaps side blisters wrapped in paper and stacked atop a counter at lower left. After numerous teething problems early on, the Bell plant was now churning out bombers at the rate of two per day and would do so until war's end without letup. (Kennesaw State University Archives.)

Not only was the B-29 the biggest and fastest bomber built during World War II, it also boasted the widest wingspan at 141 feet, 3 inches—nearly half the length of a football field. An unloaded Superfortress weighed 74,000 pounds. Once bombs, gasoline, and crew were loaded, its target weight was 120,000 pounds but often was closer to 140,000. This photograph gives a good view of the wing's flaps, which were of a type known as Fowler flaps. Now common, they were unusual on big planes in the 1940s. Flaps catch air and thereby give the wing additional lift during takeoff and landing. The pilot would retract the flaps back into the wing during cruising. (Kennesaw State University Archives.)

America's industrial muscle, which had lain mostly dormant during the long years of the Great Depression, proved unstoppable once awakened to provide the materials needed to wage war. Seen here are a dozen Superfortresses lined up on the assembly line—and there were no doubt an equal number in a similar near-ready state on the Bell plant's other line. The men and women in this picture are working on the motors and the gunners' turrets. This photograph may have been taken from the plant mezzanine but more likely was shot from atop a scaffold similar to that seen several pages earlier. (Kennesaw State University Archives.)

Dozens of completed nose sections, tails, and fuselages await final assembly, their aluminum skin gleaming under the plant's fluorescent lights. The plant had a crew who did nothing but replace burned-out bulbs. They would begin their day at one end of the plant and make their way to the other end—then would reverse course and replace the bulbs that had burned out in the meantime. (Kennesaw State University Archives.)

Workers commuted to Bell by foot, by trolley, and in many cases, despite wartime rationing, by car. The main lot at the plant, seen here, held 3,600 cars, many of which arrived via brand-new Cobb Parkway—Georgia's first four-lane divided highway—or equally new South Cobb Drive. The B-1 building is at left. (Bill Kinney.)

The Bell plant operated around the clock, with night-shift workers getting paid a premium. Many workers, though, said the pace usually was slower after dark. But thanks to the miles and miles of fluorescent lights overhead, it was never really "dark" at the Bell complex, as this photograph attests. The shot makes the plant seem almost ghostly, with few workers immediately apparent. (Bill Kinney.)

The first Bell-built B-29 finally rolls toward the door of the Marietta plant. Another 667 would follow it out by the late summer of 1945. This first plane and the next 13 were built mostly by hand because of Boeing's failure to provide the needed plans, tools, and machinery for the startup of assembly-line production. (Bill Kinney.)

There wasn't much of a crowd on hand as the first Bell-built B-29 rolled out of the giant hangar door at the end of the Marietta plant in November 1943. But Bell and its initial cadre of workers had achieved the near-impossible by building a copy of the world's most technologically advanced and complex airplane in a matter of just five months, despite delays caused by hundreds of engineering change-orders and shortages of parts and materials. The very first Superfortress, the experimental Boeing-built XB-29, had not flown until September 1942, and the Marietta engineers who built this plane had never even seen a B-29 until July 1943, when an experimental version built by Boeing landed at nearby Rickenbacker Field. Bell's achievement is even more impressive when one remembers that the ground-breaking for the Marietta plant had taken place just a year and a half earlier on March 30, 1942. (Bill Kinney.)

Four

TAKING FLIGHT

Despite the delays in building the plant, finding sufficient workers, and getting production fully under way, planes were rolling out of the Bell plant at the rate of one a day by mid-1944, a figure that increased to two a day by the following summer. The War Department, which earlier had tried to pare back production at Marietta so scarce materials could be used by other B-29 plants, reversed course and awarded Bell a $200-million contract for another 300 Superfortresses.

After leaving the main assembly building, the planes were flight tested then processed through the B-3 and B-4 hangars, where armaments, radios, and radar were installed.

And midway through the plant's run, it began producing a variant of the Superfortress known as the B-29B. That model was an effort to lighten and thereby add speed and/or bomb capacity to the plane. In part, it was a realization that Superfortresses with a full combat load of 20,000 pounds of bombs and almost 9,500 gallons of 100-octane aircraft fuel were so heavy that they were having trouble safely taking off. And in part, it was a reaction to a change in bombing tactics. The B-29s were now attacking Japan at very low altitudes (5,000 feet) instead of very high ones (30,000 feet) in order to achieve greater accuracy and results. The B-29B did away with all the turret guns and gunners except for the tail gunner. In an earlier effort to save weight, it was decided that all B-29s would fly without camouflage paint. The net result of such measures was a savings of nearly 10 tons.

B-29s finally went into service in large numbers in the Pacific in mid-1944, cheering workers in the plants who were building them and acting as an incentive for them to work even harder.

The first Bell-built B-29 Superfortress rolls out of the Marietta plant in November 1943, the culmination of five months of intensive labor by the plant's then-skeleton workforce and, before that, a year's worth of round-the-clock construction to transform cotton fields into an airfield and the South's biggest industrial complex. (Bill Kinney.)

Another view from overhead of the first Bell-built B-29 was taken at about the same time as the other shot on this page and from the same vantage point atop the plant as the photograph on page 78. Planes did not fly out of the plant in the literal sense, or even use their propellers to taxi out. Rather they were pulled by tractor. (Bill Kinney.)

Bell's first Marietta-built B-29 first flew on November 4, 1943, just days after its rollout. It had the tarmac all to itself in this photograph—a state of affairs that was not to last long. Also that fall, the plant finally went into full production mode after having been hampered since the beginning by shortages and continual design changes in the plane. (Bill Kinney.)

A trio of spanking-new B-29s basks in the bright Georgia sun in another shot taken from the Bell plant's roof. In less than a year, these three would be soaring high over the Pacific, each carrying thousands of pounds of bombs toward the Japanese home islands. (Bill Kinney.)

Above is a close-up of a B-29's tail and below another having its vertical stabilizer being craned into position. The tail of a B-29 was crammed with equipment and a separate compartment for the tail gunner, who sat behind bullet-resistant glass armed with a 20-millimeter cannon and two .50-caliber machine guns. But because they had separate trajectories, it was near impossible to achieve a simultaneous hit on an enemy fighter, so later B-29s were built without the cannons. In 1945, Pacific bomber commander Gen. Curtis LeMay decreed a switch to low-altitude bombing because of the severe high-altitude winds prevailing over Japan. And because most enemy fighter attacks were from the rear, he ordered plants to build the B-29B, which did away with all except the tail guns, thereby shedding weight and adding speed. (Both Bill Kinney.)

Once a B-29 exited the assembly building, it was pulled along to the hangar-like B-3 (paint shop) building along the plant's flight apron and then ultimately to the B-4 (preflight) building. There it was checked out in minute detail by Bell inspectors and then by inspectors from the Army Air Forces. If everything was satisfactory, it was then prepped for a test flight. Seen above are the engines revving up for the first time, one by one. After the test flight or flights, and after any problems had been checked out and logged into the plane's record, a pilot from the Army Air Force ultimately would fly the ship on to its next destination. (Both Bill Kinney.)

The Bell ground crew "runs one through" a preliminary flight test. If the blocks in front of the landing gear are any indication, this Superfortress isn't taking off anytime soon. This picture provides a good sense of just how massive the B-29's propellers were. At nearly 17 feet in circumference, they were taller than two NBA-sized centers standing on one another's shoulders. (Bill Kinney.)

Pictured from left to right are Bell engineer ? Nelson, Army Air Forces operations chief Maj. Stephen P. Dillon, and Bell chief test pilot ? Dow studying a checklist before a test flight. Development of the B-29 began under the auspices of the Army Air Corps, which six months before Pearl Harbor became the Army Air Forces. The U.S. Air Force was created by act of Congress in 1947. (Bill Kinney.)

From left to right, pilot Bloyer, pilot Cannon, flight engineer Haupmann, radio engineer Mitchell, flight mechanic Webster, and flight engineer Calkins prepare to subject a new Superfortress to a flight test. Cannon has what appears to be a Bell logo on his leather jacket. (Bill Kinney.)

Seen here are nine Superfortresses in the process of being gassed up, with the B-3 (paint shop) building in the background. A Bell fire truck is on hand, "just in case." By late fall of 1944, the Bell plant was producing bombers at the rate of about one per day. And by June 1945, they were rolling out at the rate of two a day. (Bill Kinney.)

A quartet of Superfortresses is parked on the test apron, with Kennesaw Mountain, site of a bloody battle during Sherman's Atlanta Campaign during the Civil War, visible in the distance at left. A bit closer on the hill in the distance are some of what became known as "Bell houses"—hundreds of homes built to house Bell workers on streets with names like Victory Drive and Aviation Road. (Bill Kinney.)

The test apron appears cluttered with B-29s in this shot looking out one of the big hangar doors. The B-1 main assembly building had one of the largest doors in the world when it was built, if not the largest. It measured 300 feet wide by 45 feet high and, even more remarkable for the time, could be opened and closed by sections. (Bill Kinney.)

This shot from the winter of 1944–1945 shows Superfortresses lined up in front of the B-4 preflight hangar. The plant's startup and initial output had been so slow that the Army Air Force tried to cut back Bell's production schedule so scarce supplies and materials could be redirected to the other plants building the plane, but company president Larry Bell successfully fended off such moves. (Bill Kinney.)

Georgia showers left the test apron so wet one can almost see the planes' reflections in the puddles. After blocking the War Department's attempts to cut production in Marietta, Larry Bell fought for and won a $200-million contract to build an additional 300 B-29s over the 400 the company was already expected to manufacture. (Bill Kinney.)

A Superfortress takes off from the airstrip in Marietta. Aside from actual combat, taking off while carrying a load of bombs was one of the most dangerous tasks for a B-29—one that caused the loss of many aircraft and many airmen in the Pacific theater. B-29s were designed for a gross takeoff weight of 120,000 pounds, but with a full load of gas and bombs, their weights often approached 140,000, taxing their engines. (Kennesaw State University Archives.)

Thirteen Superfortresses are on the ground, and another soars overhead in Marietta. It is possible this photograph is a composite, blending the sunny scene on the ground (note the deep shadows under the planes) and the heavy cumulus clouds above. The B-29 broke new ground in its flight manual, which required the crew to frequently recalculate takeoff and landing speeds according to weight, elevation, and temperature. (Kennesaw State University Archives.)

The rollout of this Superfortress (above) was accompanied by an entourage of plant workers and a small flag waving gaily from its tail. The reason for all the fuss is uncertain, but it is possible that this is Bell bomber No. 100, which, seen in the picture at right, was denoted as such when it came off the assembly line. By this time, the plant was well on its way not just to meeting its production targets but exceeding them. Meanwhile, now that the kinks were out, the cost per plane was going down. Bell and the other B-29 manufacturers built the planes under cost-plus-fixed-fee contracts. The B-29 was the most expensive weapons system of World War II at $3 billion, costlier even than the Manhattan Project ($2.5 billion). (Both Bill Kinney.)

The giant propellers on one Superfortress frame another on the flight apron. Bell was getting $240,000 for each B-29 it manufactured late in the war, which represented its cost of materials, wages, and salaries plus the fixed-fee percentage it received for managing the program, minus any advance payments. Bell was not reimbursed for the cost of such "government-furnished equipment" as engines, radar, landing gear, radio gear, weaponry, etc. Neither did Bell have to pay for construction of the plant, runway, or the land on which they sat. Those costs were assumed by taxpayers. (Bill Kinney.)

B-29s are shown over the Bell airstrip. In addition to its other distinctions, the Superfortress was the first aircraft to carry an onboard computer. Its Central Fire Control system, which guided the machine guns in its five gun turrets, consisted of five interconnected electronic analog computers. Each turret was controlled by its own computer, which made corrections for temperature, altitude, airspeed, range, and the acceleration of the attacking plane. The higher the altitude, the less resistance a bullet has; and the lower the temperature, the denser the air, which also affects the bullet's trajectory. Likewise, the faster the plane's speed, the farther the bullets must be deflected upwind to hit a target from broadside. Each gunner also had secondary control of the other guns, if need be. If the system was out of order, the gun could be fired manually. (Both Bill Kinney.)

A gleaming Superfortress takes off with the plant and Kennesaw Mountain in the distance. Early models of the B-29 built by Boeing wore olive drab and grey camouflage paint. But it soon was realized that despite their sleek appearance, fully loaded B-29s had difficulty achieving sufficient airspeed, which in turn caused engines to overheat and risk catastrophic fire. The solution was to save weight by leaving the planes unpainted. (Bill Kinney.)

Here is a B-29 with an experimental Bell fighter nestled under its wing, the XP-77. This was one of only two prototypes built of the XP-77, which never acquired an official name. Its design favored the use of "non-strategic" materials, such as wood. But it proved hard to fly and was underpowered. Its development was terminated in December 1944. (Kennesaw State University Archives.)

This Bell P-63 Kingcobra fighter is dwarfed by a B-29 and illustrates what a huge challenge building the Superfortress was for Bell, which previously had built only small planes like the P-39 Airacobra. The P-63 Kingcobra was an update of the P-39 Airacobra, and most of the 3,300 Bell built in Buffalo, New York, were sent to the Soviet Union. (Bill Kinney.)

A Superfortress glides high over the runway and a quartet of Bell P-63 Kingcobras down below. This photograph is believed to be a triple composite concocted by Bell's photo lab, blending shots of the runway scene, an airborne B-29, and the cumulus clouds. (Kennesaw State University Archives.)

Flight operations officer Maj. Stephen P. Dillon was one of the test pilots in Marietta and is seen above at the controls of a B-29. Test pilots sometimes do more than fly. In 1947, he was a passenger on a test flight for the Convair-built P-36 Peacemaker bomber in Fort Worth, Texas, when the hydraulic strut in the landing gear exploded just after takeoff. He parachuted out over a nearby air force base, then drove back to Bell's test field in time to commandeer a radio and guide the bomber pilot in for a safe crash landing. Robert Morris, at left, was another Bell test pilot. The Purdue University grad and flying enthusiast began his aviation career as a salesman for Piper Aircraft, worked as a barnstorm pilot, and later flew sightseeing planes over Niagara Falls before being hired by Bell. (Both Kennesaw State University Archives.)

In leather jacket with jaunty mustache is Bell test pilot Duke Krantz. Boeing's chief test pilot, Eddie Allen, died in 1942 in an unsuccessful attempt to save the B-29 prototype on its second flight after an engine caught fire just after takeoff and quickly burned through the wing. All 11 members of the Boeing test crew died when it crashed into a meatpacking plant, along with 18 workers on the ground. (Kennesaw State University Archives.)

Army Air Forces Lt. Col. William Altenburg was another flight operations officer at the Bell plant. The Kansas City native was a graduate of Bowdoin College in Maine and had studied at Harvard Business School before going in uniform. He was a test pilot flying B-26 heavy bombers and A-26 light bombers at the Glenn-Martin plant in Baltimore prior to coming to the Bell plant in Marietta. (Kennesaw State University Archives.)

Col. Jack Millar Jr., of Marietta, and the Bell-built "Georgia Peach" flew supplies to China from India over the Himalayas. The perilous route was nicknamed "The Hump," explaining the camel insignias on his plane's nose. On June 15, 1944, he led the first-ever land-based bombing mission against Japan. It also was the longest bombing mission in history to that point at 14 hours, pushing men and machines to the limits of endurance. He wrote his parents the next day in a letter published in the *Marietta Journal*, "God really was my co-pilot. . . . Even though it was pitch dark, we had to put on our dark glasses to prevent the searchlights from blinding us. . . . An enemy fighter passed above our nose and we saw the flames spitting from his guns, but they were wide and missed us, thank goodness." After the war, he was the sole survivor when his B-29 was hit by lightning and crashed. He later earned a doctorate and taught at Florida State University. (Kennesaw State University Archives.)

A Superfortress towers over a nearby car in this unusual portrait. Note how the plane's front tires appear nearly as tall as the automobile. The B-29, like most modern jetliners, featured "tricycle" landing gear—wheels under the nose and wings rather than under the wings and tail. That makes it easier to taxi and easier to apply the brakes without having the plane nose over on the runway. (Bill Kinney.)

The tail section, or "empennage," of a B-29 stands guard over a row of its sisters on the Bell tarmac. Late in the war, Gen. Curtis LeMay ordered a low-altitude bombing offensive and, to save weight, did away with all but the tail gunner and tail armaments. The top, side, and belly turret guns were replaced with broomsticks in the hopes that Japanese fighter pilots wouldn't notice the actual guns were missing. (Bill Kinney.)

Comedian Bob Hope was at the peak of his career during World War II and spent much of the war performing on USO tours for the troops and at war bond rallies. It was one of the latter that brought him to the Bell plant in November 1944. He is seen here with the zaniest of his sidekicks, bushy-mustached comedian Jerry Colonna. The performance took place one day after Bell learned that plant manager Carl Cover had been killed when the plane he was piloting on a business trip crashed in Dayton, Ohio. The news cast a pall on the plant and led to a somewhat more subdued performance from Hope than usual. The standing-room-only performance took place on a platform set up just in front of the ample wing of a Superfortress on the assembly line. (Bill Kinney.)

Five

VISITORS AND VIPS

The Bell plant attracted a parade throughout the war of the famous, the near famous, and the then famous but now forgotten. They came from Hollywood, from the battlefields, from the War Department, from the media, and from the world of politics. And by the thousands, they came from Marietta and Atlanta and countless other towns around North Georgia to tour the plant on family days.

Most of the "names" and war heroes who came did so to sell war bonds. Meanwhile, Washington was focused on ramping up production at the plant, which had gotten off to a slow start. It began to catch up in late 1944, and by 1945, the plant was churning out bombers in a steady stream. Among the visitors was four-star general Hap Arnold, commander of the Army Air Forces and one of the visionaries who in the late 1930s had foreseen the need for a very long range, very heavy bomber like the B-29.

Others who came to Bell included World War I fighter ace Eddie Rickenbacker, after whom the airfield at the plant was named; the governors of Georgia and nearby states; syndicated newspaper columnists like Drew Pearson and radio commentators like H. V. Kaltenborn; sports stars like legendary golfer Bobby Jones; Hollywood starlets with more sex appeal than apparent talent; singer and movie actor Al Jolson of *The Jazz Singer*; "America's Sweetheart," silent-screen actress Mary Pickford; and comedian Bob Hope, who uncorked a memorable performance with his zany entourage at a bond rally staged in front of a B-29 on the plant's floor.

Also passing through the plant's huge doors were ordinary men and a few women whose service and sacrifices at the front had made them heroes. Among them was one young "Angel" who fell in love with the newspaper reporter assigned to follow her that day on her tour and who wound up marrying him.

As always, Bell's photographers captured it all.

Bell Aircraft namesake Larry Bell is pictured at a patriotic rally at the Marietta plant. Note the flags of the Allies in the background. A pioneer of the American aviation industry, he formed Bell Aircraft in 1935 in Buffalo, New York, which built the P-39 Airacobra and P-63 Kingcobra fighters during World War II as well as the B-29. Bell later developed the X-1, the first fighter to break the sound barrier. (Bill Kinney.)

Plant manager Jimmie Carmichael (left with cane) tours plant with war manpower director Paul McNutt as Leo Wolfe looks on. Carmichael was hit and dragged by a car at age 15, damaging his spine, nearly killing him and leaving him in pain the rest of his life. Carmichael as Cobb County attorney helped lay the groundwork for the plant and in 1944 was hired to manage it. (Bill Kinney.)

World War I fighter ace, Medal of Honor winner, and Indy 500 driver Eddie Rickenbacker (third from left with a group examining a pressure bulkhead) was key as president of Eastern Airlines in helping Cobb afford what became Rickenbacker Field. By the time this picture was taken at Bell in 1944, he had recently survived a near-fatal plane crash just south of Atlanta as well as 24 days in a life raft in the Pacific. (Kennesaw State University Archives.)

Bell workers raised $1,500 for the March of Dimes during this drive. From left to right are Georgia governor Ellis Arnall, plant manager Carmichael, drive chairman William Jenkins, and national drive head Basil O'Connor. Bell installed a special elevator in the B-2 administration building to help Carmichael access his second-floor office. Carmichael and Bell proudly went out of their way during the war to hire the disabled. (Bill Kinney.)

Above, at left, is Gen. Hap Arnold, commander of the Army Air Forces. He was an early and ardent advocate of the B-29 and suffered a heart attack in May 1944 brought on by problems associated with the plane. He was promoted to five-star rank in late 1949 and is considered the "father" of the U.S. Air Force. He's seen touring the plant with Bell vice president and plant manager Omer Woodson, center, and Larry Bell. Then there was Maj. Gen. Bennett Meyers, at center with the mustache in the picture below. Deputy chief of army procurement during the war, he was sent to prison in 1947 after investigators discovered he had pocketed thousands of dollars as secret owner of a war plant. Arnold testified against him at his trial. Meyers is flanked by, from left to right, Col. William Altenburg, Julius Domonkos, Warren Clarke, Woodson, and Gen. William Knudsen. (Both Bill Kinney.)

Lt. Gen. William "Big Bill" Knudsen (left) and Army Air Forces Col. Charles O'Connor of the plant examine a B-29 motor. Knudsen knew a thing or two about motors, having spent three years as president of General Motors in the late 1930s. As an expert on mass production, the Danish-born Knudsen was commissioned a three-star general by President Roosevelt in 1942 and worked as a trouble-shooter and consultant for the War Department. (Bill Kinney.)

Capt. Harry Collins (left) was the original general manager of the Bell plant. He is seen with chairman Donald Nelson (center) of the War Production Board (WPB) and Colonel O'Connor as they look at one of the remote-control gunnery mechanisms that later would be installed in the B-29. The WPB was set up to manage the production and allocation of such items as heating oil, gasoline, metals, plastic, and rubber during the war. (Bill Kinney.)

It wasn't just generals who came, but generals' wives as well. Pictured above is future first lady Mamie Eisenhower, wife of Allied commander Dwight Eisenhower, who has removed her white glove in order to sign the guest register in the B-2 lobby. At left is Everett Thomas. At right is Marjorie McKeown Clay, wife of future four-star general Lucius Clay, who was instrumental in steering what became Rickenbacker Field to Marietta. Below, Mrs. Courtney Hodges admires a B-29 model held by plant manager Carmichael. Hodges's husband enlisted in the army as a private after flunking out of West Point and as a four-star general commanded the First Army during the Battle of the Bulge. A ticker tape parade in his honor was held on Peachtree Street in Atlanta in late May of 1945. (Both Bill Kinney.)

Legendary golfer Bobby Jones (second from right) presents a check to plant manager Carmichael (with cane). At their sides are Georgia Power Company executives. Though no longer playing competitively, Jones retired for good in 1948 after being diagnosed with syringomyelia. The fatal fluid-filled cavity in his spinal column caused pain and paralysis and appears to already have been bothering him when this picture was taken, based on his awkward stance. (Kennesaw State University Archives.)

CNN was still far in the future during World War II, but the plant was visited by some of the biggest radio news stars of the day, among them reporter and commentator H. V. Kaltenborn. He is seen here at the far right talking with Jimmie Carmichael (with cane). The remaining men, from left to right, are Georgia governor Ellis Arnall; Carl Cover, the plant's second manager who died in a 1944 plane crash; future governor M. E. Thompson; and E. J. Englebert. (Kennesaw State University Archives.)

Pictured above standing in the bomb bay of a B-29 are, from left to right, Chip Robert, ? La Cossett, Gov. Ellis Arnall and his son Alvan, muckraking syndicated columnist Drew Pearson, his wife, Luvie Pearson, and ? Robert. Arnall was one of Georgia's most progressive governors (1943–1947) of modern times and did away with its harsh chain-gang system, but he lost popularity for his moderate views on race. Pearson's column, "Washington Merry-Go-Round," was the most widely syndicated column in the country for decades. In the photograph below, a group of dignitaries watches as a young worker "blows up" an astrodome for a Superfortress. From left to right are Mildred Arnall, ? Broughton, an unidentified Bell worker, North Carolina governor and future U.S. senator Joseph Broughton, Governor Arnall, Omer Woodsen, and Col. Charles Collins. (Both Bill Kinney.)

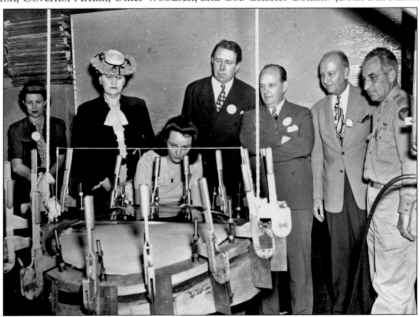

Strapped into parachutes in preparation for a spin on a B-29 are, from left to right, John Chiles, Atlanta mayor William B. Hartsfield, Dick Hawkins, and Jimmy Winn. Hartsfield was a key figure in the development of aviation in Georgia. He was among the first to see air transportation as key to the city's future and chose the site for the airport that now bears his name. Meanwhile, motoring through the plant by scooter are, from left to right, Jimmy Robinson, U.S. senator Walter George of Georgia, and Jimmie Carmichael. George resigned from the Georgia Supreme Court to run for Senate in 1922 and was the longest-tenured member of that body when he retired in 1957. George broke with President Roosevelt over his opposition to the New Deal, causing FDR to campaign unsuccessfully in the Democratic Primary for the defeat of his fellow Democrat. (Both Kennesaw State University Archives.)

Are they looking a gift mule in the mouth? These members of the Bell board of directors not only inspected the plant while in town, but they also appear to have given this mule a good going over after it pulled them in a buggy from the plant to a nearby Smyrna restaurant, Aunt Fanny's Cabin. (Kennesaw State University Archives.)

Adm. Jonas H. Ingram (center) was a football star at the Naval Academy, earned the Congressional Medal of Honor at Veracruz, Mexico, in 1914, and became commander of the Atlantic Fleet in November 1944. He later was commissioner of the All-American Football Conference until it merged with the National Football League in 1949. Note the propeller blade to the right of him. From left to right are Col. William Altenburg, Ingram, and general manager Carl Cover. (Kennesaw State University Archives.)

Lt. Mildred Dalton of Jefferson, Georgia, was one of 77 army nurses christened "the angels of Bataan and Corregidor." They worked in an open-air hospital on Bataan, were captured on Corregidor, and nearly starved to death in a Japanese prison camp. Her big smile here visiting Bell on a war bonds drive soon after her release helped captivate the reporter covering her for the *Atlanta Constitution*, Marietta native Bruce Manning—who soon became her husband. (Bill Kinney.)

These soldiers touring the Bell plant were all patients at Lawson General Hospital, a Veterans Administration hospital built on the site of World War I's Fort Gordon in nearby Chamblee on what later became the site of present-day Peachtree-DeKalb Airport. Note the empty pant legs and sleeves in this picture. (Bill Kinney.)

The original inscription on this photograph identifies these soldiers as "heroes of Bastogne," from the desperate Battle of the Bulge. Seen here by the tail of a B-29 are, from left to right, Private First-class Long, Corporal Cox, Sergeant Ford, Staff Sergeant Vail, Private First-class Ball, Captain Lemonn of the 101st Airborne Division, and Corporal Biggers. (Bill Kinney.)

The Second Air Force was set up in the Pacific Northwest and served as an air defense/training organization for bomber crews and their replacements. Contingents of its officers visited the Bell plant in March 1945 and again in May, getting better acquainted with the B-29B update. (Bill Kinney.)

At left is Dr. Corydon Wassell, a forgotten hero of World War II. A former missionary to China, he was a navy doctor at war's outbreak on Java in the Pacific. The navy ordered non-ambulatory patients left behind, but Wassell shepherded them safely to Australia, a feat made into a 1944 movie, *The Story of Dr. Wassell* starring Gary Cooper. Wassell is seen with Jimmie Carmichael (center) and Col. ? Millay. (Bill Kinney.)

Bell workers dug deep for the Army-Navy Relief Fund throughout the war. This picture shows a B-29 with its nose plastered with dollar bills donated by the plant's employees. The guard at left is holding up a folded dollar bill. Often such efforts were part of well-organized "drives," but this one was more spontaneous. (Bill Kinney.)

"Everybody's Buying War Bonds But Me . . . and you know what I am!" reads the sign on the unfortunate mule, and that pretty much sums up the attitude most people had toward buying war bonds and supporting army-navy relief during the war—it was their patriotic duty. (Bill Kinney.)

These starlets had sex appeal galore with which to sell war bonds, which is what brought them to Bell. In white is Shirley Patterson, an actress in the 1943 Batman serials who later starred in *It! The Terror From Space*. At right is Annabella, who starred opposite Henry Fonda in *Wings of the Morning* and was married for a decade to Tyrone Power. (Bill Kinney.)

Bob Hope is "On the Road to Bell," so to speak, as part of a huge war bond rally. He is seen in both pictures here with a member of his comic entourage, comedienne Barbara Allen, in character as man-hungry spinster "Vera Vague." In real life, she had studied at the Sorbonne in Paris but for stage and screen specialized in playing the ditzy Miss Vague. In an interesting twist, she costarred in *Rosie the Riveter* in 1944, a wartime comedy in which four female defense plant workers share a house with four male workers. The women and men worked different shifts but soon fight about which sex is entitled to the house at which times—and romance ensues. (Both Bill Kinney.)

The parade of celebrities pushing war bonds was not limited to sexy starlets and wisecracking comedians. Bell workers got a dose of the classics when star baritone Robert Weede (right) of the Metropolitan Opera in New York City performed in the plant. It was no doubt the biggest "hall" he ever played—so big he had to use a microphone. War bond rallies were a staple of life during World War II across the country. The bonds were touted as "loans" to the government from the public in lieu of a tax increase. But in actuality, they went on sale prior to Pearl Harbor and were meant to serve as a hedge against price inflation by taking money out of circulation. (Bill Kinney.)

Al Jolson, the most dynamic singer and entertainer of his era, starred in the first hit talking motion picture, 1929's *The Jazz Singer*. He did USO shows during the war and contracted malaria entertaining the troops in North Africa, necessitating the removal of a lung in 1943. But he had recovered in time to visit Bell in the summer of 1944 during the fifth war bond drive. (Bill Kinney.)

Atlanta native Jane Withers was one of the biggest child movie stars of the 1930s and early 1940s. She had just turned 18 when she returned to Georgia on a war bond tour and visited the Bell plant. She is seen here standing on a chair in a plant cafeteria as she entertains the crowd. It is unclear why Bell's photographers later cropped out a chunk of the picture's foreground. (Bill Kinney.)

Although in later years the Bell/Lockheed plant hosted numerous family-oriented military air shows open to the public, that concept was still in the future during World War II. What it offered instead were "family days," in which Bell employees and their families were invited to tour the inside of the plant. (Kennesaw State University Archives.)

Silent-screen movie legend Mary Pickford (right), also known as "America's Sweetheart," had met her second husband, fellow screen star Douglas Fairbanks, during a World War I bond drive. Though her film career ended with the onset of "talkies," she still had the star power to tour the country selling bonds during World War II. Pickford is seen here with Bell guard Mae Everett. (Bill Kinney.)

Thousands of Bell workers' family members flooded into the plant for Family Day in 1944 and got their first up-close look at a Superfortress. Previously, the only ones they had seen were high overhead. And for most of those touring the plant, it was the first time they had ever been inside an industrial plant. (Bill Kinney.)

Bell's black workers, or "colored" as they were referred to, brought their families on Family Day as well. But in keeping with the customs of the time, they toured the plant separately. About 2,000 blacks worked at Bell at its peak. But most were limited to less desirable jobs. (Bill Kinney.)

There were plenty of extracurricular activities at Bell to provide entertainment and boost morale. In addition to bowling leagues, baseball, softball, basketball, and other team sports, there were special dances, including one Bell sponsored at the Atlanta Municipal Auditorium that featured swing star Louis Prima in September 1944. There were also beauty contests like this one, which named one belle "Miss Bell Bomber." (Bill Kinney.)

The aptly named Mary Etta Hobbs was a riveter at Bell. She posed outside the plant in front of a blossoming dogwood tree in the spring of 1945, rivet gun in hand. The Bell photographer's original notation on the picture was "Georgia Peach." On her lapel is her Bell photo ID badge. (Kennesaw State University Archives.)

This sea of humanity surged into the plant on Family Day in 1944—some 100,000 in all. That was the equivalent of nearly three times Cobb County's 1940 population and a strong indication of the effect the opening of the Bell plant had on Marietta and its environs. The plant drew workers not only from Marietta and Atlanta, but from all over North Georgia and even from as far away as eastern Alabama and western North Carolina—quite a commute in the pre-interstate highway era. For most of the Bell workers and their families, with memories of the Great Depression still vivid, the plant offered the best job—and the best paying one—they had ever had. (Bill Kinney.)

Six

MISSION ACCOMPLISHED

After a shaky start, the Bell plant by early 1945 had become the industrial powerhouse that company president Larry Bell had long envisioned. None then knew it, but the pattern had been set that the plant would follow for most of the next 60-plus years.

First, though, came the inevitable closing when World War II ended following the dropping of a pair of atomic bombs by (non-Bell-built) B-29s. Within weeks, the government had cancelled Bell's B-29 contract, and by January 1946, all Bell's workers were gone. Its manufacturing equipment was retained, however, and machinery from other war plants was brought to Marietta and stored.

The outbreak of the Korean War led the Pentagon to reopen the plant to refurbish World War II–vintage Superfortresses, which had spent the intervening years parked in the Texas desert. But this time, the government bypassed Bell in favor of Lockheed, which had built B-17 bombers during the war, to run the Marietta plant.

Lockheed (now Lockheed-Martin) spent the rest of the cold war era building such aviation stalwarts at the plant as the C-130 Hercules, C-5 Galaxy and C-141 StarLifter cargo planes, the B-47 Stratojet bomber, and the F-22 Raptor fighter.

Plant manager Jimmie Carmichael ran for governor in 1946 and won more popular votes than his rivals but failed to gain a majority under Georgia's "county-unit system," an electoral-college-type setup designed to keep power in the hands of rural interests that later was declared unconstitutional by the U.S. Supreme Court. He then went to work for Atlanta-based Scripto, Inc., which he built into the world's largest supplier of pencils and ballpoint pens. He died at age 62 in 1972.

As for the tens of thousands of men and women who worked at Bell during the war, many finished their careers with Lockheed. Others took their newfound skills out into the workplace, and many of the Rosies devoted their postwar lives to raising families and working in the home. Their numbers now have dwindled greatly, but they retain fond memories of their contributions toward building the bomber that won the war.

B-29s were rolling out of the plant at the rate of two a day by the spring of 1945. Here a new Superfortress is being towed past the B-4 building, where they were inspected, radar and radio gear installed, and their engines were tested. Atop the brick tower on the corner was the flight control center. (Bill Kinney.)

Concern and anxiety were apparent as these Bell workers listened to news reports about the D-Day landings in Normandy on June 6, 1944. Loudspeakers were set up in the courtyard area between the B-1 (main assembly) and B-2 (administration) buildings so workers on break could monitor the latest news. (Bill Kinney.)

Judging by the pocket protectors in the shirts of a couple of these gentlemen, it is likely they are engineers. Bell was unique among B-29 plants in that it used "loft" engineering—that is, its engineers produced full-scale blueprints, which then were converted into templates for the plant's fabrication shops. The process was slow but made it easier to train workers, an important factor for Bell's largely untrained workforce. (Aviation Museum of Marietta.)

Jubilation reigned on V-E Day, May 8, 1945, when victory over Nazi Germany was announced. Pictured is a reporter from Atlanta radio station WGST (wearing the armband) interviewing plant employees. But more hard work and more brutal fighting still remained—the kind for which the B-29 was explicitly designed. (Bill Kinney.)

"Thumper" was a Marietta-built B-29 that saw early service in the skies over Japan; then after completing 40 missions, it was sent back home for a war bond drive. The bombs painted on its nose represent those 40 missions, while the 26 Japanese flags represent the number of enemy planes it had shot down. Unfortunately, most of the "Thumper" nose painting was cropped from the original picture. (Bill Kinney.)

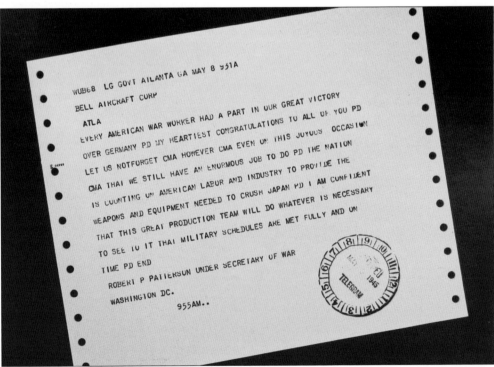

The text of this telegram from Undersecretary of the Army Robert Patterson was shared with employees when it arrived on V-E Day: "Every American had a part in our great victory. . . . Let us not forget, however, even on this joyous occasion, that we still have an enormous job to do. The nation is counting on American labor and industry to provide the weapons needed to crush Japan." (Bill Kinney.)

The B-29 Liaison Committee meets in Atlanta. Presiding at the head of the table (in front of the window) is Larry Bell. This committee included representatives of the four companies building the B-29 (Boeing, Bell, North American, and Glenn Martin Company), major subcontractors, and the War Department. Its job was to set and keep a schedule for B-29 production. (Bill Kinney.)

In the spring of 1945, a new B-29 is framed by dogwood blossoms held in front of the photographer's off-camera assistant. But by late summer, production was being scaled back as it became obvious the end of the war might be near. Bell originally had experienced difficulty hiring workers because many feared the jobs would end when the war did. Now, with the war winding down, it appeared that might in fact be the case. (Bill Kinney.)

Bell workers were all smiles on V-J Day, August 14, 1945, when victory over Japan was announced. Celebrations spontaneously broke out all over the world, and the Bell plant was no exception. The Japanese surrender was spurred by the dropping of two atomic bombs by B-29s. Though neither the "Enola Gay" (Hiroshima) nor "Bock's Car" (Nagasaki) was built by Bell, they were identical to those that were. (Bill Kinney.)

Two weeks after Hiroshima, Bell laid off 8,000 workers. Soon only a skeleton crew was left. This moody photograph taken atop the flight control center on the B-4 building is undated, but it gives a good idea of how vast the plant is and how empty it can seem. The people on the tarmac below are just dots and the vehicle and P-39 in the distance are not much larger. (Kennesaw State University Archives.)

A chapter in aviation and Southern industrial history was closing—but others were about to open. The Bell plant stood nearly empty until 1951, when Lockheed won a government contract to refurbish B-29s for use in the ongoing Korean War. Since then, the old Bell plant has been in continuous operation, manufacturing thousands of copies of the C-130 Hercules, C-141 StarLifter, C-5 Galaxy, F-22 Raptor, and others. (Bill Kinney.)

In 1997, a ramshackle remnant of a B-29 was found in South Carolina, restored, and put on display at Dobbins Air Reserve Base adjacent to the Bell plant. It was rechristened "Sweet Eloise," after Eloise Strom, who worked at the plant during the war and whose son led the restoration. Posing at the dedication are Strom, in black just beneath her name, and other former Bell workers. (*Marietta Daily Journal* photograph.)

www.arcadiapublishing.com

Discover books about the town where you grew up, the cities where your friends and families live, the town where your parents met, or even that retirement spot you've been dreaming about. Our Web site provides history lovers with exclusive deals, advanced notification about new titles, e-mail alerts of author events, and much more.

MADE IN THE USA

Arcadia Publishing, the leading local history publisher in the United States, is committed to making history accessible and meaningful through publishing books that celebrate and preserve the heritage of America's people and places. Consistent with our mission to preserve history on a local level, this book was printed in South Carolina on American-made paper and manufactured entirely in the United States.

This book carries the accredited Forest Stewardship Council (FSC) label and is printed on 100 percent FSC-certified paper. Products carrying the FSC label are independently certified to assure consumers that they come from forests that are managed to meet the social, economic, and ecological needs of present and future generations.

FSC
Mixed Sources
Product group from well-managed
forests and other controlled sources

Cert no. SW-COC-001530
www.fsc.org
© 1996 Forest Stewardship Council

Find Your Place in History.